Behold the Light

∿

by Shellie Rushing Tomlinson   art by Nicole Seitz

RIPPLES FROM PROVIDENCE

To
_____

From
_____

Date
_____

RIPPLES FROM PROVIDENCE

Copyright © 2024 Shellie Rushing Tomlinson
www.ShellieT.com

Copyright © 2024 art by Nicole Seitz
www.nicoleseitz.com

All rights reserved. No part of this book may be reproduced in any manner whatsoever without written permission except in the case of brief quotations embodied in critical articles and reviews.

First printing 2024

To my kids and their kids,
keep your eyes on the Light.
~Keggie

Now there were in the same country shepherds living out in the fields, keeping watch over their flock by night. And behold, an angel of the Lord stood before them, and the glory of the Lord shone around them, and they were greatly afraid.

Then the angel said to them, "Do not be afraid, for behold, I bring you good tidings of great joy which will be to all people. For there is born to you this day in the city of David a Savior, who is Christ the Lord. And this will be the sign to you: You will find a Babe wrapped in swaddling cloths, lying in a manger."
Luke 2:8-12 NKJV

'Twas the night before the very first Christmas,

and all through
the universe
not an angel was singing
not even
one verse.

The stars were hung
in the sky all aglow

hushed and waiting
for destiny's show.

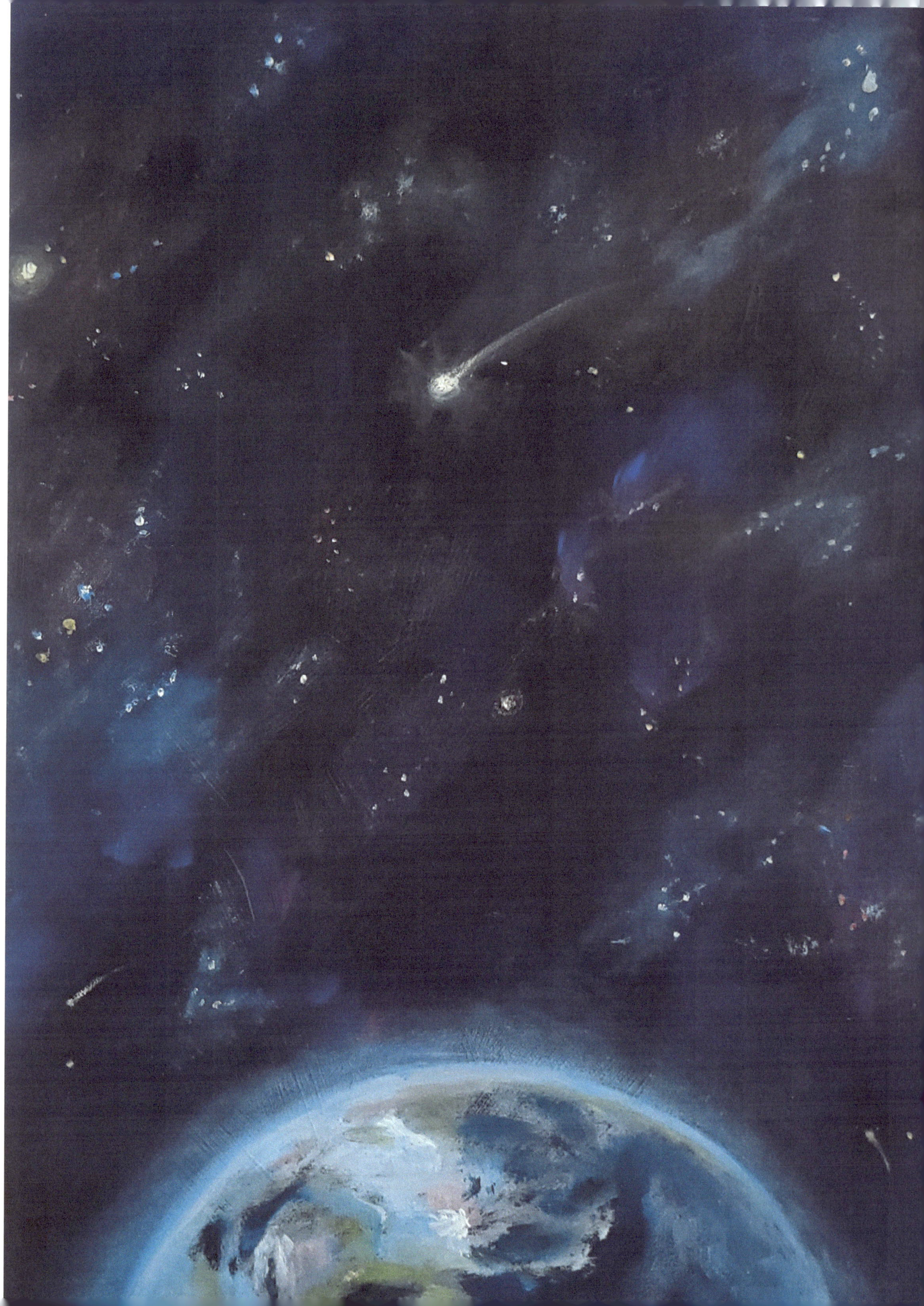

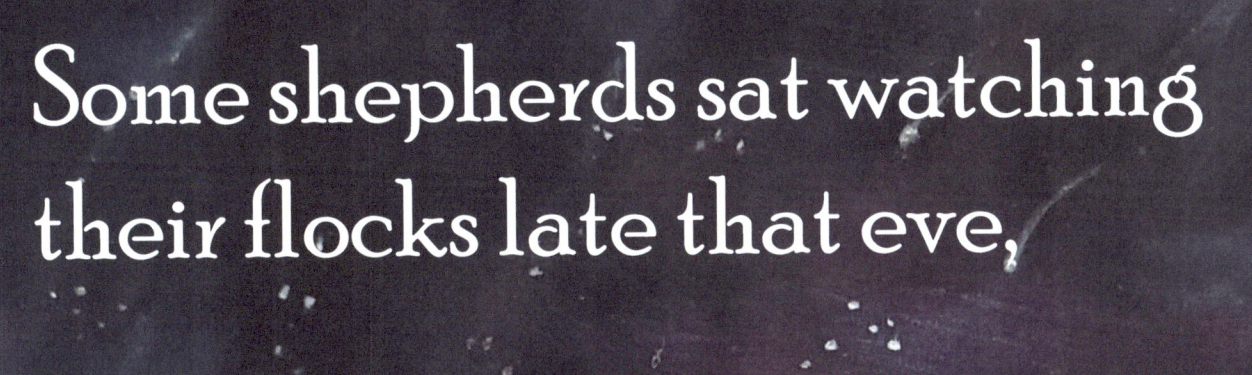

Some shepherds sat watching their flocks late that eve,

snuggled deep in their robes since the day took its leave.

And God, seated high in the heavens above, was planning a gift from his infinite LOVE.

When way up in the sky,
a great star came to shine,
and the shepherds fell back
from the wondrous sign.

For there in the heavens
came the angels to sing
of the birth of the CHRIST,
the prophesied king.

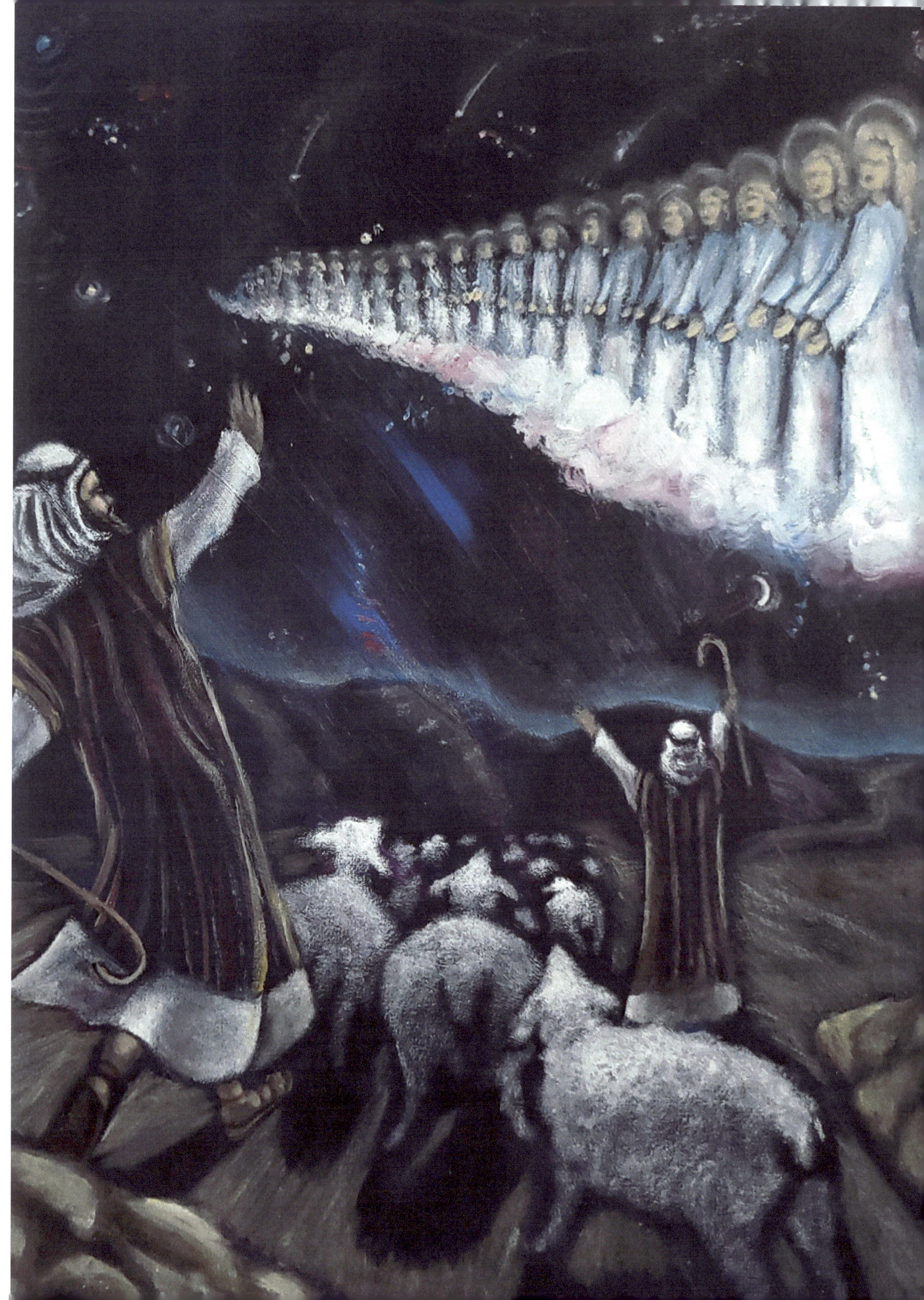

With a great star to guide them
the shepherds took flight

to find the small child
on this O Holy Night.

Above a stable
the star came to rest,
and the shepherds
bowed
low
and offered their best.

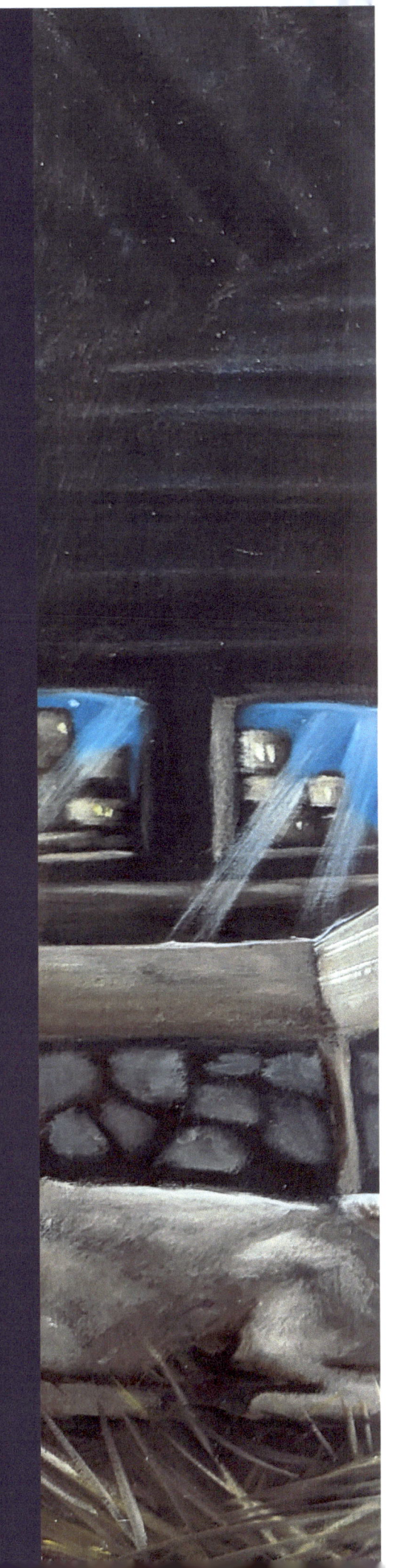

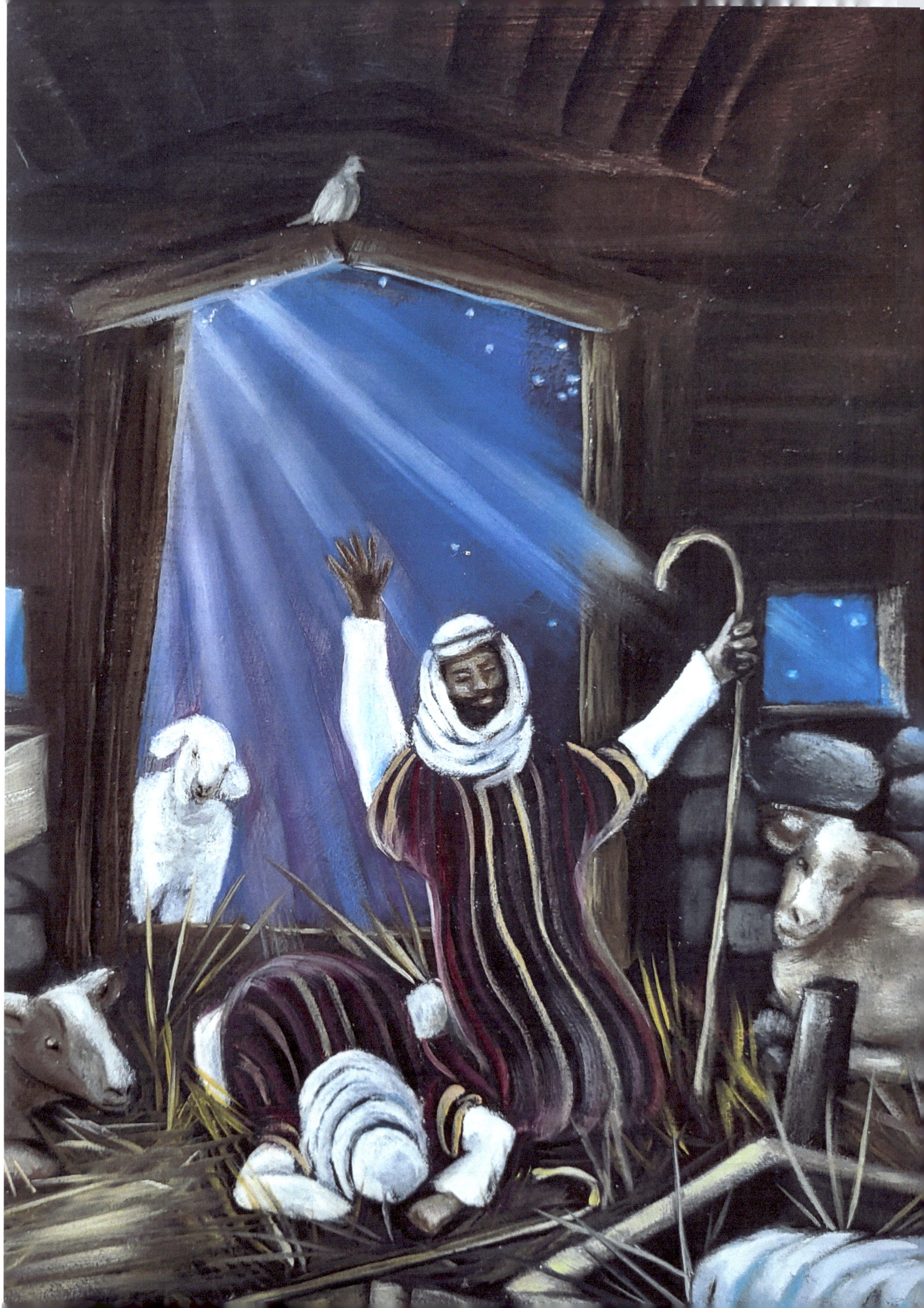

For there in the manger
with hay for a bed,
Immanuel lay sleeping
as the angel
had said.

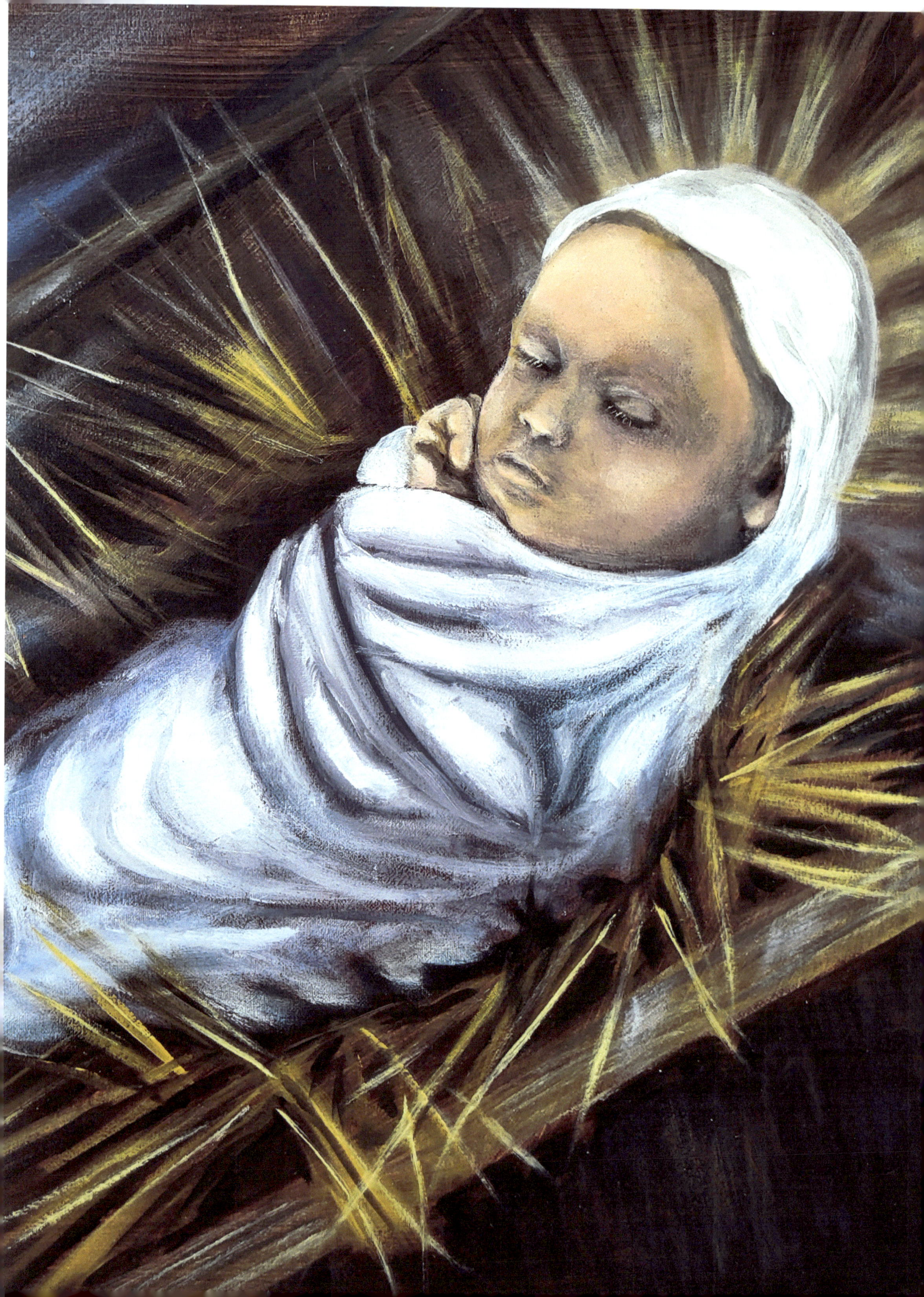

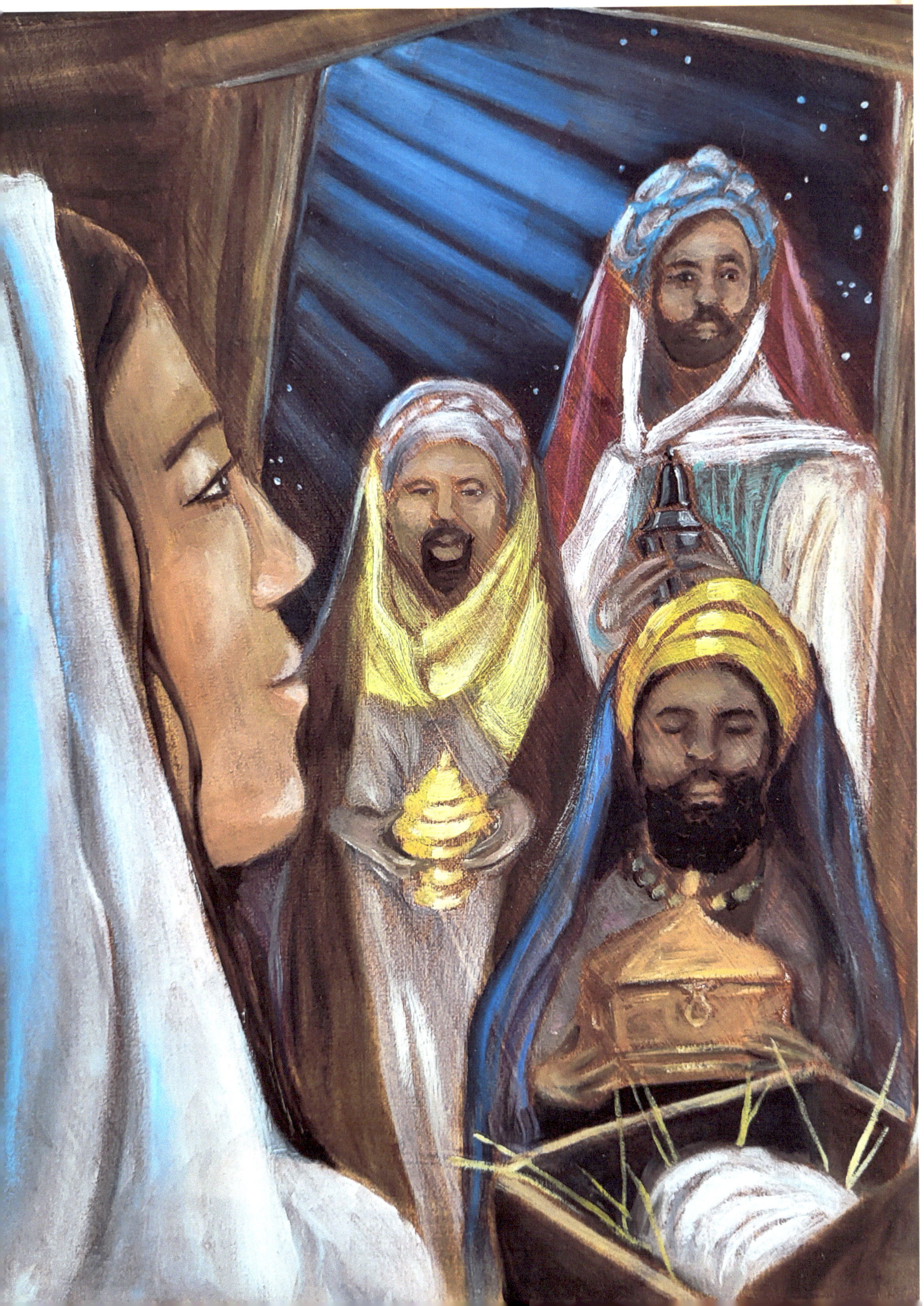

With gifts
   and with WONDER
came wise men, three,
to worship the baby
    on bended
        knee.

Treasures they lay
at the infant's feet,
frankincense,
 gold, and myrrh
  so sweet.

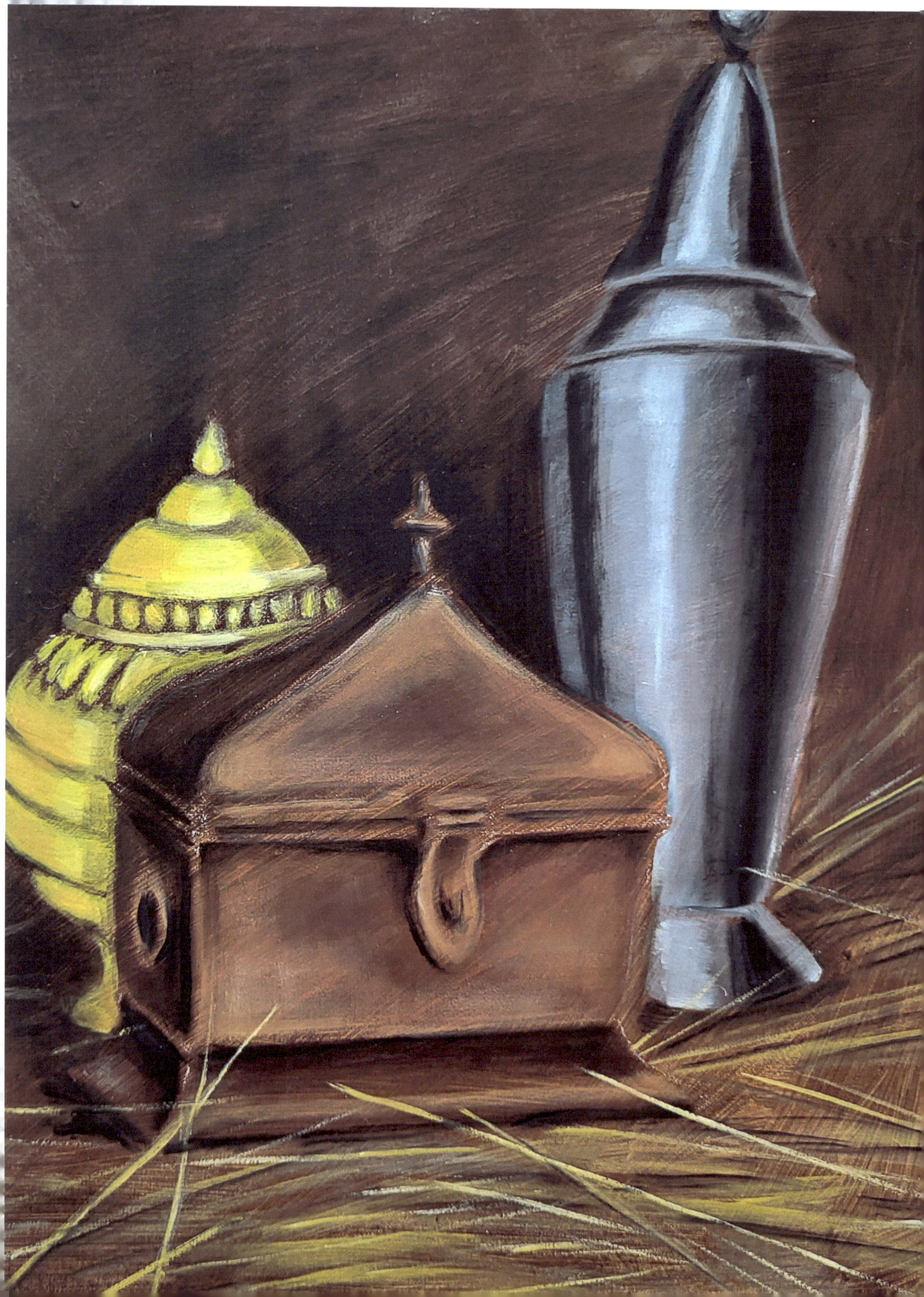

Mary, his mother,
with Joseph, her mate,
beheld it all,
    marveling
at their chosen fate.

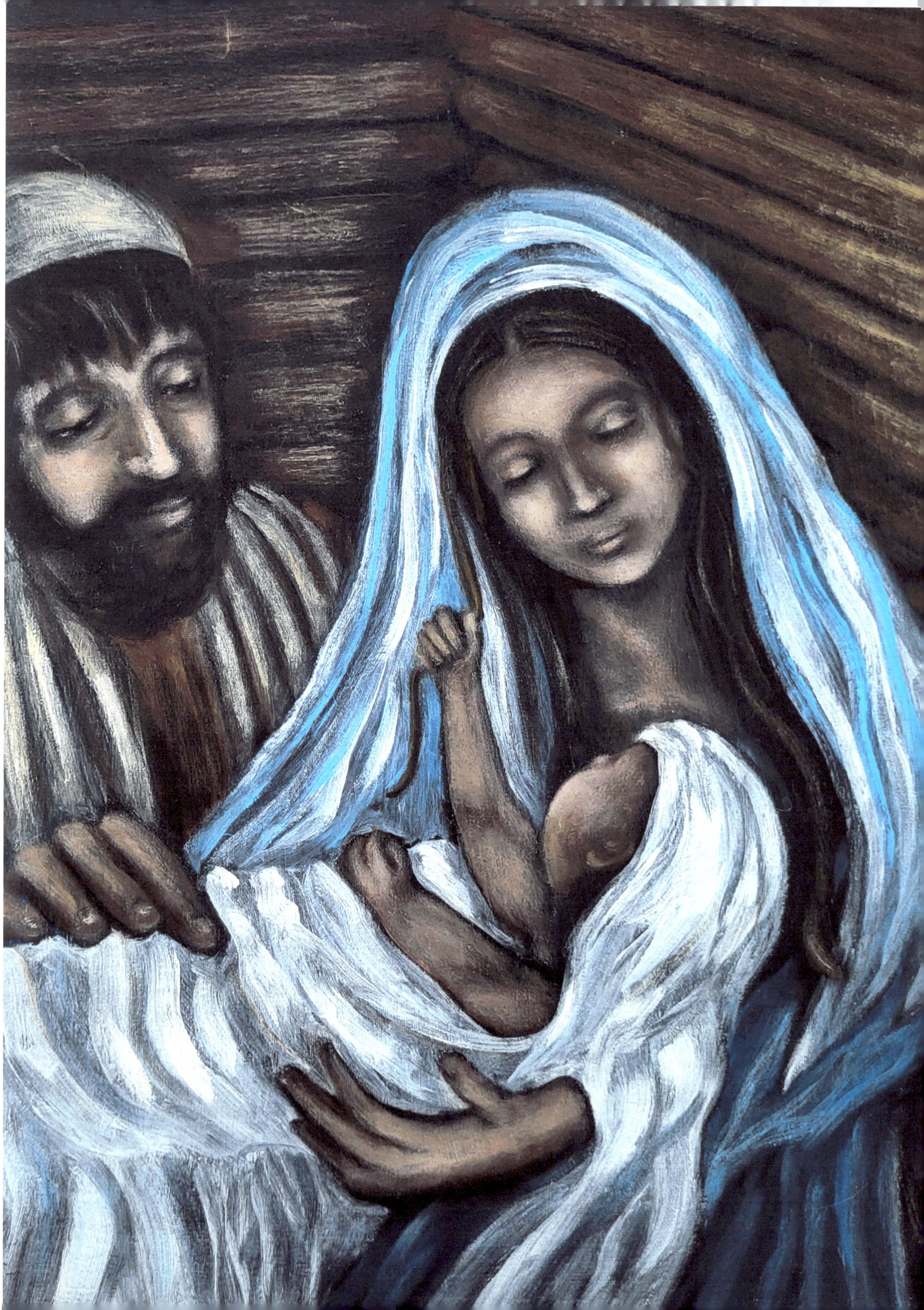

His hands,
they were stretching
far into the night.

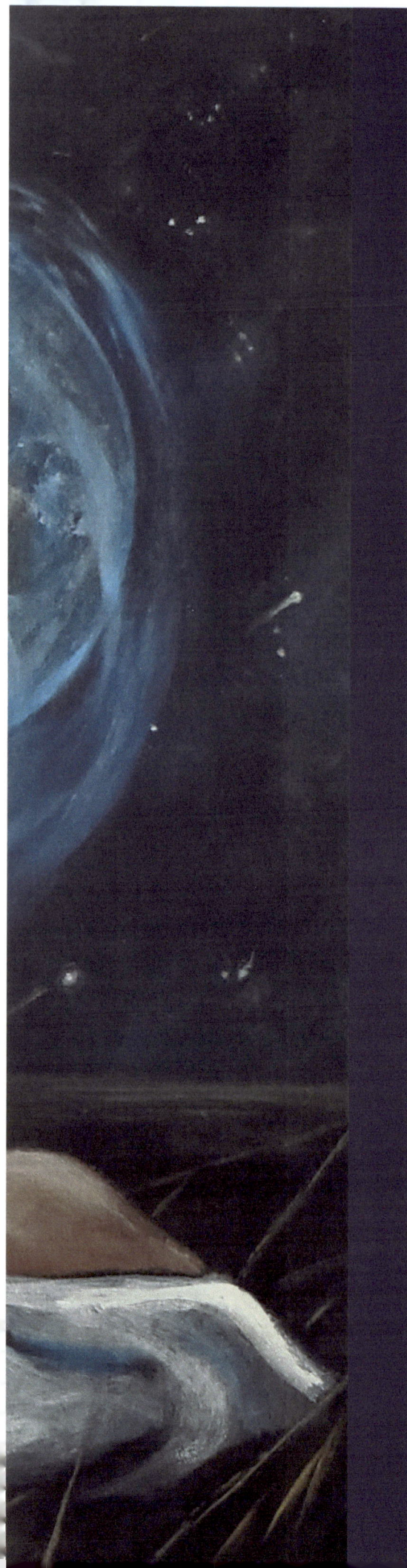

His eyes
full of wisdom,
his face filled with
light.

His message for men,
the angels did say,
was PEACE on earth
and GLORY to stay.

As the animals
looked on
and the world stood
still,
God smiled at this scene
and spread his goodwill.

To all those below,
BEHOLD THE LIGHT!

Merry Christmas to all
and to all a good night.